I0480262

Checklist for Starting a Small Business

Must Know Must Do Before Setting Up a Business

MEIR LIRAZ

Published by BizMove
www.bizmove.com

Copyright © 2017 Meir Liraz

All rights reserved.

ISBN: 1974217299
ISBN-13: 978-1974217298

Table of Contents

MEIR LIRAZ

1. Introduction

Owning a business is the dream of many people ... starting that business converts your dream into reality. But there is a gap between your dream and reality that can only be filled with careful planning. As a business owner, you will need a plan to avoid pitfalls, to achieve your goals and to build a profitable business.

The "Checklist for Starting a Small Business" is a guide to help you prepare a comprehensive business plan and determine if your idea is feasible, to identify questions and problems you will face in converting your idea into reality and to prepare for starting your business.

Operating a successful small business will depend on:

a practical plan with a solid foundation;

dedication and willingness to sacrifice to reach your goal;

technical skills; and

basic knowledge of management, finance, record keeping and market analysis.

As a new owner, you will need to master these skills and techniques if your business is to be successful.

2. Identify Your Reasons

As a first and often overlooked step, ask yourself why you want to own your own business. Check the reasons that apply to you.

1. Freedom from the 9-5 daily work routine.

2. Being your own boss.

3. Doing what you want when you want to do it.

4. Improving your standard of living.

5. Boredom with your present job.

6. Having a product or service for which you feel there is a demand.

Some reasons are better than others, none are wrong; however, be aware that there are tradeoffs. For example, you can escape the 9 to 5 daily routine, but you may replace it with a 6 a.m. to 8 p.m. routine.

3. A Self-Analysis

Going into business requires certain personal characteristics. This portion of the checklist deals with you, the individual. These questions require serious thought. Try to be objective. Remember, it is your future that is at stake!

Personal Characteristics

Please answer with a 'yes' or 'no':

1. Are you a leader?

2. Do you like to make your own decisions?

3. Do others turn to you for help in making decisions?

4. Do you enjoy competition?

5. Do you have will power and self discipline?

6. Do you plan ahead?

7. Do you like people?

8. Do you get along well with others?

Personal Conditions

This next group of questions though brief is vitally important to the success of your plan. It covers the physical emotional and financial strains you will encounter in starting a new business.

Are you aware that running your own business may require working 12-16 hours a day six days a week and maybe even Sundays and holidays?

Do you have the physical stamina to handle the workload and schedule?

Do you have the emotional strength to withstand the strain?

Are you prepared if needed to temporarily lower your standard of living until your business is firmly established?

Is your family prepared to go along with the strains they too must bear?

Are you prepared to lose your savings?

Personal Skills And Experience

Certain skills and experience are critical to the success of a business. Since it is unlikely that you possess all the skills and experience needed you'll need to hire personnel to supply those you lack. There are some basic and special skills you will need for your particular business.

By answering the following questions you can identify the skills you possess and those you lack (your strengths and weaknesses).

Do you know what basic skills you will need in order to have a successful business?

Do you possess those skills?

When hiring personnel will you be able to determine if the applicants' skills meet the requirements for the positions you are filling?

Have you ever worked in a managerial or supervisory capacity?

Have you ever worked in a business similar to the one you want to start?

Have you had any business training in school?

If you discover you don't have the basic skills needed for your business will you be willing to delay your plans until you've acquired the necessary skills?

4. Finding a Niche

Small businesses range in size from a manufacturer with many employees and millions of dollars in equipment to the lone window washer with a bucket and a sponge. Obviously the knowledge and skills required for these two extremes are far apart but for success they have one thing in common: each has found a business niche and is filling it.

The most critical problems you will face in your early planning will be to find your niche and determine the feasibility of your idea. "Get into the right business at the right time" is very good advice but following that advice may be difficult. Many entrepreneurs plunge into a business venture so blinded by the dream that they fail to thoroughly evaluate its potential.

Before you invest time effort and money the following exercise will help you separate sound ideas from those bearing a high potential for failure.

5. Is Your Idea Feasible?

Identify and briefly describe the business you plan to start.

Identify the product or service you plan to sell.

Does your product or service satisfy an unfilled need?

Will your product or service serve an existing market in which demand exceeds supply?

Will your product or service be competitive based on its quality selection price or location?

Answering yes to any of these questions means you are on the right track; a negative answer means the road ahead could be rough.

6. Market Analysis

For a small business to be successful the owner must know the market. To learn the market you must analyze it a process that takes time and effort. You don't have to be a trained statistician to analyze the marketplace nor does the analysis have to be costly.

Analyzing the market is a way to gather facts about potential customers and to determine the demand for your product or service. The more information you gather the greater your chances of capturing a segment of the market. Know the market before investing your time and money in any business venture.

These questions will help you collect the information necessary to analyze your market and determine if your product or service will sell.

1. Do you know who your customers will be?

2. Do you understand their needs and desires?

3. Do you know where they live?

4. Will you be offering the kind of products or services that they will buy?

5. Will your prices be competitive in quality and value?

6. Will your promotional program be effective?

7. Do you understand how your business compares with your competitors?

8. Will your business be conveniently located for the people you plan to serve?

9. Will there be adequate parking facilities for the people you plan to serve?

This brief exercise will give you a good idea of the kind of market planning you need to do. An answer of no indicates a weakness in your plan so do your research until you can answer each question with a "yes".

7. Planning Your Start-up

So far this checklist has helped you identify questions and problems you will face converting your idea into reality and determining if your idea is feasible. Through self-analysis you have learned of your personal qualifications and deficiencies and through market analysis you have learned if there is a demand for your product or service.

The following questions are grouped according to function. They are designed to help you prepare for "Opening Day".

Name and Legal Structure

1. Have you chosen a name for your business?

2. Have you chosen to operate as sole proprietorship partnership or corporation?

Your Business and the Law

A person in business is not expected to be a lawyer but each business owner should have a basic knowledge of laws affecting the business. Here are some of the legal matters you should be acquainted with:

1. Do you know which licenses and permits you may need to operate your business?

2. Do you know the business laws you will have to obey?

3. Do you have a lawyer who can advise you and help you with legal papers?

4. Are you aware of

Occupational Safety and Health requirements?

Regulations covering hazardous material?

Local ordinances covering signs snow removal etc.?

Tax Code provisions pertaining to small business?

Workmen's Compensation laws?

8. Protecting Your Business

It is becoming increasingly important that attention be given to security and insurance protection for your business. There are several areas that should be covered. Have you examined the following categories of risk protection?

Fire

Theft

Robbery

Vandalism

Accident liability

Discuss the types of coverage you will need and make a careful comparison of the rates and coverage with several insurance agents before making a final decision.

9. Business Premises and Location

1. Have you found a suitable building in a location convenient for your customers?

2. Can the building be modified for your needs at a reasonable cost?

3. Have you considered renting or leasing with an option to buy?

4. Will you have a lawyer check the zoning regulations and lease?

Merchandise

Have you decided what items you will sell or produce or what service(s) you will provide?

Have you made a merchandise plan based upon estimated sales to determine the amount of inventory you will need to control purchases?

Have you found reliable suppliers who will assist you in the start-up?

Have you compared the prices quality and credit terms of suppliers?

Business Records

Are you prepared to maintain complete records of sales income and expenses accounts payable and receivables?

Have you determined how to handle payroll records tax reports and payments?

Do you know what financial reports should be prepared and how to prepare them?

10. Finances

A large number of small businesses fail each year. There are a number of reasons for these failures but one of the main reasons is insufficient funds. Too many entrepreneurs try to start and operate a business without sufficient capital (money). To avoid this dilemma you can review your situation by analyzing these three questions:

1. How much money do you have?

2. How much money will you need to start your business?

3. How much money will you need to stay in business?

The chart below will help you answer the second question: How much money will you need to start your business? The chart is for a retail business; items will vary for service construction and manufacturing firms.

The answer to the third question (How much money will you need to stay in business?) must be divided into two parts: immediate costs and future costs.

Start-up Cost Estimates

Decorating, remodeling - _____

Fixtures, equipment   - _____

Installing fixtures, equipment - _____

Services, supplies - _____

Beginning inventory cost - _____

Legal, professional fees - _____

Licenses, permits - _____

Telephone utility deposits - _____

Insurance - _____

Signs - _____

Advertising for opening - _____

Unanticipated expenses - _____

Total start-up costs - _____

From the moment the door to your new business opens a certain amount of income will undoubtedly come in. However this income should not be projected in your operating expenses. You will need enough money available to cover costs for at least the first three months of operation. The chart below will help you project your operating expenses on a monthly basis.

Expenses for one month

Your living costs - _____

Employee wages - _____

Rent - _____

Advertising - _____

Supplies - _____

Utilities - _____

Insurance - _____

Taxes - _____

Maintenance - _____

Delivery/transportation - _____

Miscellaneous - _____

Total expenses - _____

Now multiply the total of the chart above by three. This is the amount of cash you will need to cover operating expenses for three months. Deposit this amount in a savings account before opening your business. Use it only for those purposes listed in the above chart because this money will ensure that you will be able to continue in business during the crucial early stages.

By adding the total start-up costs to the total expenses for three months (three times the total cost on The chart above) you can learn what the estimated costs will be to start and operate your business for three months. By subtracting the totals of the charts from the cash available you can determine the amount of additional financing you may need if any. Now you will need to estimate your operating expenses for the first year after start-up.

The first step in determining your annual expenses is to estimate your sales volume month by month. Be sure to consider seasonal trends that may affect your business. Information on seasonal sales patterns and typical operating ratios can be secured from your trade associations.

(NOTE: The relationships among amounts of capital that you invest levels of sales each of the cost categories the number of times that you will sell your inventory (turnover) and many other items form "financial ratios." These ratios provide you with extremely valuable checkpoints before it's too late to make adjustments. In the reference section of your local library are publications such as "The Almanac of Business and Industrial Financial Ratios" to compare your performance with that of other similar businesses.

Next determine the cost of sales. The cost of sales is expressed in dollars. Fill out each month's column in dollars total them in the annual total column and then divide each item into the total net sales to produce the annual percentages. Examples of operating ratios include cost of sales to sales and rent to sales.

11. After Start-up

The primary source of revenue in your business will be from sales but your sales will vary from month to month because of seasonal patterns and other factors. It is important to determine if your monthly sales will produce enough income to pay each month's bills.

An estimated cash flow projection will show if the monthly cash balance is going to be subject to such factors as:

Failure to recognize seasonal trends;

Excessive cash taken from the business for living expenses;

Too rapid expansion; and

Slow collection of accounts if credit is extended to customers.

Use the following chart to build a worksheet to help you with this problem. In this example all sales are made for cash.

Estimated Cash Flow Forecast

	Jan.	Feb.	Mar.	Apr. (etc.)
Cash in bank (1st of month)	___	___	___	___
Petty cash (1st of month)	___	___	___	___
Total cash (1st of month)	___	___	___	___
Anticipated cash sales	___	___	___	___
Total receipts	___	___	___	___
Total cash & receipts	___	___	___	___
Disbursements for month	___	___	___	___
(rent, payments, utilities, wages, etc.)				
Cash balance (end of month)	___	___	___	___

12. Conclusion

Beyond a doubt preparing an adequate business plan is the most important step in starting a new business. A comprehensive business plan will be your guide to managing a successful business. The business plan is paramount to your success. It must contain all the pertinent information about your business; it must be well written factual and organized in a logical sequence. Moreover it should not contain any statements that cannot be supported.

If you have carefully answered all the questions on this checklist and completed all the worksheets you have seriously thought about your goal. But . . . there may be some things you may feel you need to know more about.

Owning and running a business is a continuous learning process. Research your idea and do as much as you can yourself but don't hesitate to seek help from people who can tell you what you need to know.

13. Starting a Business FAQ

To start and run a small business you must know and be many things. As one small business owner attending a conference put it: "When I came here, my business lost the services of its chief executive, sales manager, controller, advertising department, personnel director, head bookkeeper, and janitor."

This setting up business ideas guide, based on questions asked by people in small business or contemplating starting, suggests the many facets of running a small concern that each owner/manager must become familiar with.

While the answers to the questions are hardly exhaustive of any of the subjects, they provide the background for questions you may need to ask before going into business, as well as suggesting sources of answers to those questions.

Almost everyone considering it has dozens of questions about starting a small business. The only foolish questions, of course, are the questions that aren't asked. Yet, many times we don't have enough information to ask the right questions.

The questions in this guide are drawn from participants in training courses for new entrepreneurs. Most of the questioners didn't own, operate, or manage small businesses. Their questions are typical of what's on the minds of potential business owners. You may have pondered similar questions, as you thought about becoming your own boss.

The questions fell generally into areas such as the steps in setting up a business, marketing, and financing a new concern. In this guide the questions have been grouped by subject.

Answers to the questions came from experts in the various areas. These experts include a lawyer, an accountant, a bank loan officer, several small business owners, and market researchers.

These answers, it is hoped, will help you as you approach deciding on becoming a small business owner.

The questions may suggest questions that you should find answers to before you invest your money, time, and effort in a small business.

Open a Business Advice Starting Out

1. If you have money but no particular business in mind, how can you get enough information on the best business to go into?

The best way of choosing your business venture is to look at your experience and educational background. A thorough review will provide leads on the business field you should enter - do what you know best. Even more important, you must like the business field you are going to enter to bring the enthusiasm and self-confidence you need to make the business go.

2. What are the basic survival skills you need to run a business?

The basic survival skills include a working knowledge of basic record keeping; financial management; personnel management; market analysis; break-even analysis; product or service knowledge; tax knowledge; legal structures; and communication skills.

3. What special obstacles do women entering business face, and how can these obstacles be overcome?

Women are at last making inroads into business, not only as executives but as owners. There are many obstacles, chief among them the doubts that lenders, suppliers, and in some fields, customers have about women's ability to run businesses. These can be overcome with self confidence and a strong belief in your ideas. You should not be discouraged by being rebuffed by people who simply don't understand. As more and more women enter business and succeed, the process will become easier and easier.

4. What are the most important factors that cause small business failure?

There are, of course, many reasons for the failure of new small businesses. One way of looking at the causes is to remember that a new business is starting at zero momentum; newly entering a market, having to establish supplier relations, finding proper financing, and training employees. To coordinate all these facets and start them simultaneously is a tremendous job. If you don't have experience and management capability, success won't be very likely. You'll also find that under-capitalized businesses, those without enough cash to carry them through the first six months or so before the business starts making money, don't have good survival prospects. In such cases, even businesses with good management can founder.

5. If you're trying to buy a going service business, how can you figure a reasonable price for the business that takes into account goodwill and business contacts in addition to the value of equipment and inventory?

There are many methods, but basically what you're trying to do is set a value on the assets and earnings record of the firm. The simplest way is to determine the "payback period," usually two or three years. That is, the net profit for two years would equal the goodwill value. A more complicated and accurate method called the "net present value" method, is based on the cost of capital and a risk factor. For that method an accountant's help would be valuable.

6. What kind of a market study should you do before

deciding to buy a radio station?

Determining the price of any business is difficult. For a radio station specifically, you can get the figures on the total revenue of all stations in the area (that is, advertising revenue). You should also get the percentage of the total market that the station you're considering has. You must also determine the potential market for the area in advertising dollars. Finding out the total number of businesses by line and size in the area covered by the station and their advertising expenditures would give you some insight. Really, you'd study the market like this for buying any business.

7. How long does it take a new business to establish a good public image?

A good public image takes a long time to establish (and only minutes to lose). There is no set formula, but a good image depends on:

- The service, products, and customer treatment you provide;
- The market you're in;
- How you stack up against your competitors;
- The quality of your public relations and advertising programs.

If you're new to a market - and if you do what you say you're going to - you may establish an excellent reputation in 18 to 24 months.

8. How do you find a good lawyer?

As with most personal services, you must have rapport with your attorney. The best way to determine this is to talk to lawyers by phone or visit them before you make a selection. Get recommendations from friends, or your banker. You're looking for someone you can trust and who will take an interest in you and your business.

9. Do you need a lawyer to start a business?

No, but it's wise to get the best advice possible when you're starting out. An attorney is one source of the expertise you'll need to draw on.

Setting Up Business Form of Business

10. What form of business do you recommend for a new business?

Each legal form, sole proprietorship, partnership, or corporation, has its advantages and disadvantages. The one you should pick depends on your circumstances, including:

- Your financial condition,
- The line of business you're entering,
- The number of employees,
- The risk involved,
- Your tax situation.

Don't assume, if you plan a one-person business, that sole proprietorship is the way to go. See your lawyer.

The Market (Open a Business Advice)

11. How can you find out what the prevailing costs are for a service business in your market area?

One way is simply to call competitors and ask their prices. Their prices will give you a lead. You could ask competitors' customers for the same information if you didn't want to go directly to the competition.

12. How do you go about determining the market for a mail order business?

The principles of determining market share and market potential are the same no matter how large the geographical area. You must first determine a customer profile, the size of the market, and the number of competitors. You could also use a readership survey given to you by a magazine in which you intend to advertise.

Pricing

13. How do you figure markup and markdown?

Markup (markon) is the original amount that the merchandise is marked up. Markup as a percentage (also called gross margin rate) is figured as a percentage of sales. For example, say the cost of merchandise is $10 and you want a 20 percent markup; what is the selling price (SP)? By definition we know that markup as a percentage is given as a percentage of sales. Thus, our cost must be 80 percent of the selling price (100 percent selling price - 20 percent desired markup).

So, our selling price is $12.50, cost $10.00, and markup $2.50 or 20 percent of the selling price.

Markdown (discount) is a reduction of selling price below the original sale price. Assume the item is marked down to $11.25. The markdown is $1.25 or a 10 percent markdown ($1.25 markdown divided by $12.50 original selling price).

14. How would you go about establishing price guidelines for a business renting items to customers?

Pricing is based normally on a combination of cost and market competition. Trade associations are a prime source of such information.

Finances

15. What is the average expected net profit for small business?

Average net profits vary with the type of business - retail, wholesale, service, manufacturing, construction. They also vary for the type of business structure - proprietorship or corporation. Dun & Bradstreet publish ratios which give you these figures, as well as lots of very useful cost information.

16. Would you explain the meaning of "rate of return

on investment"? How is it different from net profit? Is it different from return on assets employed?

Net profit (before taxes) is basically total sales for a specific period less cost of goods and operating expenses during that period. (For a retail business, cost of goods would be your cost of merchandise sold.) Net profit is a function of both rate of return on investment (ROI) and return on total assets. ROI is net profit divided by capital invested by the owners of the company.

ROI is used to measure the effectiveness of management in attaining the owners' desired return on their investment. Generally, the larger the ROI, the more attractive a company is to potential investors.

Return on total assets is the net profit divided by total assets. This measures the net profitability of the use of all resources of the business. It is another tool for measuring management effectiveness in the use of all resources borrowed and equity.

17. Does a bank require absolute top credit references from loan applicants?

The better the credit references the greater the possibility of loan approval.

18. If I estimate my start-up cost at $50,000 and can't put up anywhere near the $25,000 that I've been told is what I should have for my share, am I wasting my

time even filling out a loan application?

In all probability you would be, although there are some exceptions. For example, it might be possible to get a loan under your circumstances if you were buying a business that's already operating well enough to provide sufficient profits to cover its obligations and the loan. Furthermore, if the applicant is the present manager who has made this business go, the chances of getting such a loan are much better.

Help!

19. Getting money is difficult; keeping it may be even more difficult. Where can I get assistance in managing my business?

Your accountant and bank can provide financial counseling which can be very helpful in starting and managing your business. They can also give you in valuable information on the local area and your market that can be critical in making decisions in your business.

14. How To Solve Problems

As the owner of your own business you deal with problems on an almost daily basis. Being familiar with effective Problem Solving Techniques can dramatically affect the growth of your business.

Although you find solutions to your problems, many businessmen and women are not really skilled in the methods of problem solving, and when solutions fail, they fault themselves for misjudgment. The problem is typically not misjudgment but rather a lack of skill.

This guide instructs you in some problem solving techniques. Crucial to the success of a business faced with problems is your understanding of just what the problems are, defining them, finding solutions, and selecting the best solutions for the situations. This guide explains the following.

How to identify a problem. How to respond to it. The different techniques and methods used in problem-solving. How to find alternative solutions. How to select the best solution for the situation. Designing a Plan of Action. How to implement the Plan of Action. How to assess the success of the solution and the Plan of Action.

Introduction to Problem Solving Techniques

What is a problem. A problem is a situation that presents difficulty or perplexity. Problems come in many shapes and sizes. For example, it can be:

Something did not work as it should and you don't know how or why. Something you need is unavailable, and something must be found to take its place. Employees are undermining a new program. The market is not buying. What do you do to survive? Customers are complaining. How do you handle their complaints?

Where do problems come from? Problems arise from every facet of human and mechanical functions as well as from nature. Some problems we cause ourselves (e.g., a hasty choice was made and the wrong person was selected for the job); other problems are caused by forces beyond our control (e.g., a warehouse is struck by lightning and burns down).

Problems are a natural, everyday occurrence of life, and in order to suffer less from the tensions and frustrations they cause, we must learn how to deal with them in a rational, logical fashion.

If we accept the fact that problems will arise on a regular basis, for a variety of reasons, and from a variety of sources, we can:

learn to approach problems from an objective point of view; learn how to anticipate some of them; and prevent some of them from becoming larger problems.

To accomplish this, you need to learn the process of problem solving.

Here, we will instruct you in the basic methods of problem-solving. It is a step by step guide which you can easily follow and practice. As you follow this guide, you will eventually develop some strategies of your own that work in concert with the problem-solving process described in this guide.

Keep in mind, though, as you read that this is not a comprehensive analysis of the art of problem-solving but rather a practical, systematic, and simplified, yet effective, way to approach problems considering the limited time and information most business owners and managers have. In addition, some problems are so complex that they require the additional help of experts in the field, so be prepared to accept the fact that some problems are beyond one person's ability, skill, and desire to succeed.

1. Identifying The Problem

Before a problem can be solved, you must first recognize that a problem exists. Here is where your approach to problem-solving is crucial. You should not allow the problem to intimidate you. You should approach it rationally and remind yourself that every problem is solvable if it is tackled appropriately.

Fear can block your ability to think clearly, but if you:

1. Follow a workable procedure for finding solutions;

2. Accept the fact that you can't foresee everything;

3. Assume that the solution you select is your best option at the time; and

4. Accept the possibility that things may change and your solution fail;

you will then enter the problem-solving process rationally, You should try to view it as an intellectual exercise. Once you recognize that a problem exists, your next step is to identify the problem. First, you need to discover how the problem occurred. Ask yourself the following questions:

1. Did something go wrong?

2. Did something breakdown?

3. Were there unexpected results or outcome?

4. Is something that once worked no longer working?

Second, you need to know the nature of the problem:

1. Is it people, operational, technical, etc.?

2. Is it with a particular department, product or service, etc.?

3. Is it something tangible or intangible?

4. Is it an external or internal problem?

Third, you need to decide how significant the problem is. Based on the level of significance, you may choose to deal with the problem or not to deal with it. Sometimes what you think is a small problem, when analyzed, proves to be a major problem. The reverse is also true. To determine this, you should ask yourself the following types of questions:

1. Is it disrupting operations?

2. Is it hampering sales?

3. Is it causing conflict among people?

4. Is it an everyday occurrence or is it infrequent?

5. Is it affecting personnel and their productivity?

6. Is it common or unusual?

7. Is it affecting goals, and if yes, which ones?

8. Is it affecting customers, vendors, and any other external people?

Fourth, you should narrow down the type of problem:

1. Is it basically a problem which occurred in the past and the main concern is to make certain that it doesn't occur again?

2. Is it a problem which currently exists and the main concern is to clear up the situation?

3. Is it a problem which might occur in the future and the basic concern is planning and taking action before the problem arises?

The answer to all of the above questions will help you focus on the true problem. You cannot effectively research the causes of a problem until you have a clear understanding of what the problem is. Sometimes, people spend many hours on what they perceive as a problem only to find out, after seeking the causes, that something else was really the problem.

In order to appropriately identify the problem and its causes, you must do some research. To do this, simply list all the previous questions in checklist form, and keeping the checklist handy, go about gathering as much information as you possibly can. Keep in mind the relative importance and urgency of the problem, as well as your own time limitations. Then interview the people involved with the problem, asking them the questions on your checklist.

After you've gathered the information and reviewed it, you will have a pretty clear understanding of the problem and what the major causes of the problem are. At this point, you can research the causes further through observation and additional interviewing. Now, you should summarize the problem as briefly as possible, list all the causes you have identified, and list all the areas the problem seems to be affecting.

Before proceeding to finding solutions, there is some additional research that could be done. If possible and if warranted, you might wish to find out:

1. What has previously been done in regards to this problem.

2. What have other companies done.

3. What formal knowledge might you need to acquire.

4. What has been learned from past experience.

5. What do experts say about the problem.

2. Roadblocks to Problem Solving

Many of us serve as our own roadblocks in solving problems. There are a variety of roadblocks to watch for in order to effectively use the technique of problem solving:

1. Watch out for old habits.

2. Check your perceptions.

3. Overcome your fears.

4. Be careful of assumptions.

5. Don't be tied to a problem; try to look at it with detachment.

6. Don't let yourself procrastinate.

7. Control your inclination for reactive solutions.

8. Control your inclination for rash solutions.

9. Avoid emotional responses and always attempt to be rational.

10. Be aware that the nature of a problem can change.

11. Do not skip steps in the problem solving process.

At this point, you are ready to check your understanding of the problem. You've already identified the problem, broken it all down into all its facets, narrowed it down, done research on it, and you are avoiding typical roadblocks. On a large pad, write down the problem, including all of the factors, the areas it affects, and what the effects are. For a better visual understanding, you may also wish to diagram the problem showing cause and effect.

Study what you have written down and/or diagrammed. Call in your employees and discuss your analysis with them. Based on their feedback, you may decide to revise. Once you think you fully understand the causes and effects of the problem, summarize the problem as succinctly and as simply as possible.

3. How to Find Solutions

There are a number of methods for finding solutions. We will describe five thinking methods below, but we recommend that you use a number of them in finding solutions. The first four methods described are unconventional and more innovative. They allow you the possibility of arriving at a novel solution. The fifth method is a more typical and straightforward method.

1. Association: There are three types of associative thinking. This type of thinking is basically a linking process either through similarity, difference, or contiguity. For example, contiguity finds solutions from things that are connected through proximity, sequence, and cause and effect. The process works as follows: List as many parts of the problem you can think of. Then giving yourself a short time limit, list as many words or ideas that have either proximity, sequence, or related cause and effect to the ones you have listed. For example, a contiguous association might be "misplaced work - cluttered desk" (proximity); "misplaced work - rushing" (sequence); "misplaced work - irate customer" (cause and effect).

Associative thinking taps the resources of the mind. It brings into focus options you might not have considered if you stuck to ideas only directly related to the problem. As a result of associative thinking, you might find other relationships embedded in the problem that will lead to a better solution.

2. Analogy: This thinking method is a way of finding solutions through comparisons. The process is based on comparing the different facets of the problem with other problems that may or may not have similar facets. An analogy might go like this: "Employees have been coming in late to work quite often; how can I get them to be at work on time? This to me is like soldiers being late for a battle. Would soldiers come late to a battle? Why not?" By, comparing the situation of workers to the situation of soldiers, you may find a solution for a way to motivate employees to come to work on time.

3. Brainstorming: This thinking method is based on a free, non-threatening, anything goes atmosphere. You can brainstorm alone or with a group of people. Most often a group of people from diverse backgrounds is preferable. The process works like this: The problem is explained to the group and each member is encouraged to throw out as many ideas for solutions as he or she can think of no matter how ridiculous or far-fetched they may sound. All the ideas are discussed among the group, revised, tossed out, expanded, etc. based on the group's analysis of them. Based on the group's grasp of the effectiveness of each idea, the best ones are selected for closer review. For example, the group of people might throw out for consideration any thoughts they might have on how to increase sales or improve profits.

4. Intuition: This mode of thinking is based on hunches. It is not, as some think, irrational. Intuition or hunches are built on a strong foundation of facts and experiences that are buried somewhere in the subconscious. All the things you know and have experienced can lead you to believe that something might be true although you've never actually experienced that reality. Use your intuition as much as possible but check it against the reality of the situation.

5. Analytical Thinking: This thinking method is based on analysis. It is the most conventional and logical of all the methods and follows a step by step pattern.

a. Examine each cause of the problem. Then for each cause, based on your direct knowledge and experience, list the solutions that logically would seem to solve the problem.

b. Check the possible solutions you arrive at with the research you have compiled on how the problem was solved by others.

Using each thinking technique, search for solutions. Keep a running list of all of them, even the ones that seem far out, too simple, or even impossible. The effect of this is to give you a rich pool of ideas that will lead you to the best solution.

4. Sorting Out the Best Solution

Go through your long list of solutions and cross-out those that obviously won't work. Those ideas are not wasted for they impact on those ideas that remain. In other words, the best ideas you select may be revised based on the ideas that wouldn't work. With the remaining solutions, use what is called the "Force Field Analysis Technique." This is basically an analysis technique which breaks the solution down into its positive effects and negative effects. To do this, write each solution you are considering on a separate piece of paper. Below the solution, draw a line vertically down the center of the paper. Label one column advantages and one column disadvantages.

Now, some more analytical thinking comes into play. Analyzing each facet of the solution and its effect on the problem, listing each of the advantages and disadvantages you can think of.

One way to help you think of the advantages and disadvantages is to role-play each solution. Call in a few of your employees and play out each solution. Ask them for their reactions. Based on what you observe and on their feedback, you will have a better idea of the advantages and disadvantages of each solution you are considering.

After you complete this process for each solution, select those solutions which have the most advantages. At this point, you should be considering only two or three. In order to select the most appropriate solution, you should check each solution against the following criteria:

Cost effectiveness; Time constraints; Availability of

manpower, material, etc.; Your own intuition.

Before you actually implement the solution, you should evaluate it. Ask yourself these questions:

1. Are the objectives of the solution sound and clear and not complex?

2. Will the solution achieve the objectives?

3. What are the possibilities it will fail and in what way?

5. The Plan of Action

Finding the solution does not mean the problem is solved. Now, you need to design a plan of action so that the solution gets carried out properly. Designing and carrying out the plan of action is equally as important as the solution. The best solution can fail because it is not implemented correctly. When designing the plan of action, consider the following:

Who will be involved in the solution; Who will be affected by the solution; What course of action will be taken; How should the course of action be presented to company employees, customers, vendors, etc.; When will it happen - the time frame; Where will it happen; How will it happen; What is needed to make it happen.

Design a plan of action chart including all the details you need to consider to carry it out and when each phase should happen. Keep in mind, though, that the best plans have setbacks for any number of reasons - from a key person being out for illness to a supplier shipping material late. So remember that your dates are only target dates. Solutions and plans of action must be flexible. Expect some things to be revised.

6. Evaluating the Plan of Action

Before you implement the plan of action, you should analyze it to see if you've considered as many of the variables as possible. Some questions you might ask yourself are:

1. Is there adequate staff to carry it out?

2. Is the plan detailed yet simple enough for those affected to know what to expect and how to carry it out?

3. Will it embarrass anyone - manager, employee, customer, vendor, etc.?

4. Is the time frame realistic and feasible?

5. Are there special conditions which may have been overlooked?

6. Who should be informed?

7. Who should be involved?

8. Who should be responsible for each aspect and/or phase?

9. Is the plan of action cost effective?

10. Does the plan have a public relations component?

7. Obstacles You May Encounter

There are a number of obstacles you may encounter when you implement your plan of action. It is, therefore, advisable that you devise ways to overcome them. Try not to allow obstacles to prevent you from reaching your goals. Some obstacles to watch for are:

1. Not receiving material and/or equipment on time;

2. Other situations which might arise and deflect your attention from this problem;

3. Procrastination;

4. A power struggle among managers and/or employees;

5. Resistance to change - a natural human condition.

Resistance to change and company-wide acceptance is typically the biggest obstacle. The best way to overcome them is to build a public relations component into your plan of action. The key question to ask yourself is, "How will I get my people to support the solution and make it work?" Some effective methods for accomplishing this are:

1. Have as many managers and employees involved in the problem solving process as possible.

2. Advertise the problem and solution to your employees through memos, newsletters, and posters, showing the advantages and disadvantages of the solution but proving it is better than the conditions which currently exist.

3. Establish a schedule of meetings where different groups of employees can be exposed to the solution and ask them for their feedback.

4. If necessary, develop a training program so that managers and employees feel competent in carrying out the solution.

5. Involve key leaders who wield impact and influence others.

The key to a successful PR campaign is involving, as much as possible, the people who are affected by the problem. The benefits of doing so is that they will understand the problem better and why the solution is an effective one. The result will be that they will be more likely to not only support your solution but also make sure that it works. Many times the solutions we select for problems don't work because employees sabotage them, not because they are not inherently good solutions. Employees may resist change, especially if they feel threatened. Involving employees will assuage their fears.

8. Simulating the Solution / Plan of Action

Before you implement the plan of action on a full scale, you should select a small group of managers and employees and role play the solution in the work setting. Observe the group as they carry out the solution and take note of:

1. How they carry out the solution;

2. Their reactions to the solution;

3. Their understanding of the solution;

4. The effectiveness of the tools they are using in carrying out the solution;

5. Their resistance to change and reverting back to the previous behaviors.

Based on what you observe, you may need to revise some of your plans.

9. Successful Implementation

To assure the successful implementation successful implementation of your solution and plan of action, remember the following:

1. Prepare your staff well in advance;

2. Train your staff well in advance;

3. Order equipment, material, etc., well in advance;

4. If necessary, hire new staff and do so well in advance;

5. Use PR at every meeting and in memos as much as possible;

6. Evaluate the effects of each phase as it is implemented and make the necessary adjustments;

7. Attempt to remain flexible and open-minded.

Evaluating the Success of Your Solution

As each phase of your plan of action is implemented, you should ask yourself whether your goals were achieved, how well they were achieved, and did it work smoothly. To check your own perceptions of the results, get as much feedback as possible from your managers and from your employees. What you may think is working may not be working well in the eyes of your people. Always remember that they are one of your most valuable tools in successfully carrying out your solution.

15. How to Determine the Feasibility Of Your Business Idea

This chapter features questions concentrating on areas you must consider seriously to determine if your idea represents a real business opportunity and if you can really know what you are getting into. You can use it to evaluate a completely new venture proposal or an apparent opportunity in your existing business.

Perhaps the most crucial problem you will face after expressing an interest in starting a new business or capitalizing on an apparent opportunity in your existing business will be determining the feasibility of your idea. Getting into the right business at the right time is simple advice, but advice that is extremely difficult to implement. The high failure rate of new businesses and products indicates that very few ideas result in successful business ventures, even when introduced by well established firm. Too many entrepreneurs strike out on a business venture so convinced of its merits that they fail to thoroughly evaluate its potential.

This checklist should be useful to you in evaluating a business idea. It is designed to help you screen out ideas that are likely to fail before you invest extensive time, money, and effort in them.

Preliminary Analysis

A feasibility study involves gathering, analyzing and evaluating information with the purpose of answering the question: "Should I go into this business?" Answering this question involves first a preliminary assessment of both personal and project considerations.

General Personal Considerations

The first seven questions ask you to do a little introspection. Are your personality characteristics such that you can both adapt to and enjoy business ownership/management?

1 Do you like to make your own decisions?

2 Do you enjoy competition?

3. Do you have will power and self-discipline?

4. Do you plan ahead?

5. Do you get things done on time?

6. Can you take advise from others?

7. Are you adaptable to changing conditions?

The next series of questions stress the physical, emotional, and financial strains of a new business.

8. Do you understand that owning your own business may entail working 12 to 16 hours a day, probably six days a week, and maybe on holidays?

9. Do you have the physical stamina to handle a business?

10. Do you have the emotional strength to withstand the strain?

11. Are you prepared to lower your standard of living for several months or years?

12. Are you prepared to loose your savings?

Specific Personal Considerations

1. Do you know which skills and areas of expertise are critical to the success of your project?

2. Do you have these skills?

3. Does your idea effectively utilize your own skills and abilities?

4. Can you find personnel that have the expertise you lack?

5. Do you know why you are considering this project?

6. Will your project effectively meet your career aspirations

The next three questions emphasize the point that very few people can claim expertise in all phases of a feasibility study. You should realize your personal limitations and seek appropriate assistance where necessary (i.e. marketing, legal, financial).

7. Do you have the ability to perform the feasibility study?

8. Do you have the time to perform the feasibility study?

9. Do you have the money to pay for the feasibility study done?

General Project Description

1. Briefly describe the business you want to enter.

_____

2. List the products and/or services you want to sell

_____

3. Describe who will useyour products/services

_____

4.Why would someone buy your product/service?

_____

5.What kind of location do you need in terms of type of neighborhood, traffic count, nearby firms, etc.?

_____

6. List your product/services suppliers.

_____

7. List your major competitors - those who sell or provide like products/services. _____

8. List the labor and staff you require to provide your products/services. _____

Small Business Set Up Requirements For Success

To determine whether your idea meets the basic requirements for a successful new project, you must be able to answer at least one of the following questions with a "yes."

1.Does the product/service/business serve a presently unserved need?

2. Does the product/service/business serve an existing market in which demand exceeds supply?

3. Can the product/service/business successfully compete with an existing competition because of an "advantageous situation," such as better price, location, etc.?

Major Flaws

A "Yes" response to questions such as the following would indicate that the idea has little chance for success.

1. Are there any causes (i.e., restrictions, monopolies, shortages) that make any of the required factors of production unavailable (i.e., unreasonable cost, scare skills, energy, material, equipment, processes, technology, or personnel)?

2.Are capital requirements for entry or continuing operations excessive?

3. Is adequate financing hard to obtain?

4. Are there potential detrimental environmental effects?

5. Are there factors that prevent effective marketing?

Starting Company Guide Desired Income

The following questions should remind you that you must seek both a return on your investment in your own business as well as a reasonable salary for the time you spend in operating that business.

1. How much income do you desire?

_____

2.Are you prepared to earn less income in the first 1-3 years?

_____

3.What minimum income do you require?

_____

4.What financial investment will be required for your business?

_____

5.How much could you earn by investing this money?

_____

6.How much could you earn by working for someone else?

_____

7.Add the amounts in 5 and 6. If this income is greater that what you can realistically expect from your business, are you prepared to forego this additional income just to be your own boss with the only prospects of more substantial profit/income in future years?

_____

8. What is the average return on investment for a business of your type? _____

Preliminary Income Statement

Besides return on investment, you need to know the income and expenses for your business. You show profit or loss and derive operating ratios on the income statement. Dollars are the (actual, estimated, or industry average) amounts for income and expense categories. Operating ratios are expressed as percentages of net sales and show relationships of expenses and net sales.

For instance 50,000 in net sales equals 100% of sales income (revenue). Net profit after taxes equals 3.14% of net sales. The hypothetical "X" industry average after tax net profit might be 5% in a given year for firms with 50,000 in net sales. First you estimate or forecast income (revenue) and expense dollars and ratios for your business. Then compare your estimated or actual performance with your industry average. Analyze differences to see why you are doing better or worse than the competition or why your venture does or doesn't look like it will float.

These basic financial statistics are generally available for most businesses from trade and industry associations, government agencies, universities and private companies and banks

Forecast your own income statement. Do not be influenced by industry figures. Your estimates must be as accurate as possible or else you will have a false impression.

1. What is the normal markup in this line of business. i.e., the dollar difference between the cost of goods sold and sales, expressed as a percentage of sales?

_____

2. What is the average cost of goods sold percentage of

sales?

_____

3.What is the average inventory turnover, i.e., the number of times the average inventory is sold each year?

_____

4.What is the average gross profit as a percentage of sales?

_____

5. What are the average expenses as a percentage of sales?

_____

6. What is the average net profit as a percent of sales?

_____

7. Take the preceding figures and work backwards using a standard income statement format and determine the level of sales necessary to support your desired income level.

_____

8. From an objective, practical standpoint, is this level of sales, expenses and profit attainable?

_____

Any Business
Condensed Hypothetical Income Statement
For year ending December 31

Item	Amount	Percent
Gross sales	773,888	
Less returns, alowances, and cash discounts	14,872	
Net sales	759,016	100.00
Cost of goods sold	382,392	50.38
Gross profit on sales	376,624	49.62
Selling expenses	41,916	5.52
Administrative expenses	28,010	3.69
General expenses	50,030	6.59
Financial expenses	5,248	0.69
Total expenses	125,204	16.50
Operating profit	251,420	33,12
Extraordinary expenses	5,200	0.69
Net profit before taxes	246,220	32.43
Taxes	46,781	6.16
Net profit after taxes	199,439	26.62

Market Analysis

The primary objective of a market analysis is to arrive at a realistic projection of sales. after answering the following questions you will be in a better positions to answer question eight immediately above.

Population

1. Define the geographical areas from which you can realistically expect to draw customers.

_____

2. hat is the population of these areas?

_____

3. What do you know about the population growth trend in these areas? _____

4. What is the average family size?

_____

5. What is the age distribution?

_____

6. What is the per capita income?

_____

7. What are the consumers' attitudes toward business like yours?

_____

8.What do you know about consumer shopping and spending patterns relative to your type of business?

_____

9. Is the price of your product/service especially important to your target market?

_____

10. Can you appeal to the entire market?

_____

11. If you appeal to only a market segment, is it large enough to be profitable?

_____

Competition

1. Who are your major competitors?

_____

2. What are the major strengths of each?

_____

3. What are the major weaknesses of each?

_____

4. Are you familiar with the following factors concerning your competitors:

Price structure?

_____

Product lines (quality, breadth, width)?

_____

Location?

_____

Promotional activities?

_____

Sources of supply?

_____

Image from a consumer's viewpoint?

_____

5. Do you know of any new competitors?

_____

6. Do you know of any competitor's plans for expansion?

_____

7. Have any firms of your type gone out of business lately?

_____

8. If so, why?

_____

9. Do you know the sales and market share of each competitor?

_____

10. Do you know whether the sales and market share of each competitor are increasing, decreasing, or stable?

_____

11. Do you know the profit levels of each competitor?

_____

12.Are your competitors' profits increasing, decreasing, or stable?

_____

13. Can you compete with your competition?

_____

Sales

1. Determine the total sales volume in your market area.

_____

2. How accurate do you think your forecast of total sales is?

_____

3. Did you base your forecast on concrete data?

_____

4. Is the estimated sales figure "normal" for your market area?

_____

5. Is the sales per square foot for your competitors above the normal average?

_____

6. Are there conditions, or trends, that could change your forecast of total sales?

_____

7. Do you expect to carry items in inventory from season to season, or do you plan to mark down products occasionally to eliminate inventories? If you do not carry over inventory, have you adequately considered the effect of mark-down in your pricing? (Your gross profits margin may be too low.) _____

8. How do you plan to advertise and promote your product/service/business? _____

9. Forecast the share of the total market that you can realistically expect - as a dollar amount and as a percentage of your market.

_____

10. Are you sure that you can create enough competitive advantages to achieve the market share in your forecast of the previous question? _____

11. Is your forecast of dollar sales greater than the sales amount needed to guarantee your desired or minimum income?

_____

12. Have you been optimistic or pessimistic in your forecast of sales? _____

13. Do you need to hire an expert to refine the sales forecast?

_____

14. Are you willing to hire an expert to refine the sales forecast? _____

Supply

1. Can you make a list of every item of inventory and operating supplies needed?

2. Do you know the quantity, quality, technical specifications, and price ranges desired?

3. Do you know the name and location of each potential source of supply?

4. Do you know the price ranges available for each product from each supplier?

5. Do you know about the delivery schedules for each supplier?

6. Do you know the sales terms of each supplier?

7. Do you know the credit terms of each supplier?

8. Do you know the financial condition of each supplier?

9. Is there a risk of shortage for any critical materials or merchandise?

10. Are you aware of which supplies have an advantage relative to transportation costs?

11. Will the price available allow you to achieve an adequate markup?

Expenses

1. Do you know what your expenses will be for: rent, wages, insurance, utilities, advertising, interest, etc?

2. Do you need to know which expenses are Direct, Indirect, or Fixed?

3. Do you know how much your overhead will be?

4. Do you know how much your selling expenses will be?

Miscellaneous

1. Are you aware of the major risks associated with your product? Service Business?

2. Can you minimize any of these major risks?

3. Are there major risks beyond your control?

4. Can these risks bankrupt you? (fatal flaws)

Starting Company Guide Venture Feasibility

1. Are there any major questions remaining about your proposed venture?

2. Do the above questions arise because of a lack of data?

3. Do the above questions arise because of a lack of management skills?

4. Do the above questions arise because of a "fatal flaw" in your idea?

5. Can you obtain the additional data needed?

7. Are you aware that there is less than a 50-50 chance that you will be in business two years from now?

16. How To Make Money With Your New Idea or Invention

New Ideas for Business, Getting Business New Idea are essential to business progress. It is very difficult, however, for innovators to get the kind of financial and management support they need to realize their ideas.

This Guide, aimed at idea people, inventors, and innovative owner-managers of companies, describes the tests every idea must pass before it makes money.

You've Got New Business Ideas? Great!

So, you've had a new business idea for an invention or an innovative way of doing something that will boost productivity, put more people to work, and make lots of money for you and anyone who back you? As you've probably heard, you're the kind of person your country needs to compete in world markets and maintain its standard of living. You're the cutting edge of the future.

You are another of those individuals on whom progress has always depended. We all know that it hasn't been huge corporations that have come up with the inventions that have revolutionized life. As the discoverer of penicillin, Sir Alexander Flemming, said, "It is the lone worker who makes the first advance in a subject: The details may be worked out by a team, but the prime idea is due to the enterprise, thought and perception of an individual." Innovators like you are business's lifeblood.

Owner-managers who have started companies on new ideas know first hand about the innovation process. They also know that you can expect to hear...

You've Got a New Business Idea? So What?

In the first place, the chances that you are the first to come up with a particular innovation are somewhere between slim and none. Secondly, even if you have come up with the better mouse trap, nobody - but nobody - is going to beat a path to your door. In fact, in the course of trying to peddle your BMT, you'll beat up plenty of shoe leather wearing paths to other people's doors. You'll stand a good chance of wearing out your patience and several dozen crying towels as well.

Well, new product failure rates are estimated conservatively to be between 50 and 80 percent. One survey of major companies with millions of dollars to spend of R & D, market research, and product advertising, and with well-established distribution systems found that of 58 internal proposals only 12 made it past initial screening. From these 12 only one successful new product emerged.

Another group set up to help innovators has found that of every 100 ideas submitted 85 have too many faults to bother with. They can be eliminated immediately. Of the remaining 15, maybe five will ever be produced. One of those might - only might - make money.

With odds like 99 to 1 against an idea being a monetary success, is it any surprise that your idea is greeted with a chorus of yawns? People - companies, investors, what have you - are basically conservative with their money. Ideas are risky.

Does that mean you should forget about your idea? Of course not. It merely means that now you're beginning to see what Edison meant, when he said, "Genius is one percent inspiration and ninety-nine percent perspiration."

Again, those of you who own small firms started on innovations are well aware of the truth of Edison's words. You've been through the hard work.

Can You Exploit Your New Business Ideas?

Although coming up with what you think is a sure-fire idea is the biggest step, it's still only the first one. You've got the other thousand miles of the journey to success still ahead of you.

Many things remain to be done before you can expect to realize the first dollar from your invention or other innovation. You should be prepared for the unhappy discovery that the end of the line for your idea may turn up well before the point you needed to reach to make money from it.

At a bare minimum, your idea will have to pass the following tests:

- Is it original or has someone else already come up with it?
- Can someone produce and distribute it if it's an invention or other product, or use it if it's a marketing innovation, a new use for an existing product or the like?
- Will it really make money? (Will someone buy it?)
- Can you protect your idea?

That seems to be a modest enough list, and it is. The problems arise from the dozens of underlying questions that must be answered before the major questions can be resolved. Here, for example, are the 33 areas that the University of Oregon's Innovation Center runs each submitted idea through to determine if it has commercial merit:

- Legality
- Safety
- Environmental Impact
- Societal Impact
- Potential Market
- Product Life Cycle
- Usage Learning
- Product Visibility
- Service
- Durability
- New Competition

- Functional Feasibility
- Production Feasibility
- Stability of Demand
- Consumer
- User Compatibility
- Marketing Research
- Distribution
- Perceived Function
- Existing Competition
- Potential Sales
- Development Status
- Investment Costs
- Trend of Demand
- Product Line Potential
- Need
- Promotion
- Appearance
- Price
- Protection
- Payback Period
- Profitability
- Product Interdependence
- Research and Development

Now that is not a modest list. However, for the moment lets ignore the 33 and look at the four broad questions.

Is Your New Business Ideas Original?

Obviously, if somebody has already come up with and produced as good an item or a better one, it would be pointless for you to pursue a similar idea any further. You'd only be wasting your time and money.

There are lots of places to look to find out. If your idea is for a consumer product, check stores and catalogs. Check trade associations and trade publication in the field into which your invention or innovation fits. Visit trade shows relevant to your idea. Look in the business and popular press. (Here, you can consult The Reader's Guide to Periodical Literature to help you in your search. Your public library has a copy.)

Don't be afraid to ask people in the field if they've ever heard of anything along the lines of your idea. In the pure idea stage it's not very likely that somebody will steal your idea - all the hard work still has to be done. Besides, you can ask general sorts of questions and keep the details of your idea to yourself if you're really anxious that your idea will be pirated. Patent rights to an idea in major foreign countries will be jeopardized by uncontrolled disclosure prior to filing a patent application in the United States.

Obviously, if what you've come up with is an invention or an idea that can be put into patentable form, you'll eventually have to make a patent search. You could do that in this early stage, but it is probably a better idea to hold off until you've taken a look at your idea in the light of the next two questions?

How Will the New Business Idea or Invention Be Produced and Distributed?

The first thought many innovators have is to take their

ideas to a big national company. Provide the dazzling idea, they think, and let the giant work out the details. After all, the national company has the money, the production capability, and the marketing know-how to make this surefire profit maker go.

Unfortunately, the big companies are almost never interested in ideas from outsiders. Whether that's because, as one innovation broker has suggested, that outside technology is "a risk, a threat," or simply because large corporations need potential sales of an item to be in the tens of millions of dollars, doesn't matter. The cold fact is that selling a big firm on your idea is in the 100,00 to 1 shot range.

On the other end of the scale, you may be able to produce some items yourself, working out of your home and selling by mail order. This method can be a good way to get started, but after a while you may find yourself getting tired of having 200,000 better mouse traps stashed in your bedroom.

To be sure, if you can start (or already have) your own company, you will be better off. It's easier to sell a company than a patent, even if the company is losing money.

Many potential buyers understand a company much better than they understand the technology of an invention. Business people usually look at the profit-and-loss possibilities differently from the way an innovator does.

Many of these business people follow what one innovator has called "the 'Anyhow' theory of economics"; We have a plant anyhow. We have a sales force anyhow. We advertise anyhow. We're smarter anyhow." Such business people also know that by the time they purchase a company most of the bugs are out of the technology and customers exist.

Between the extremes of starting your own company or having big business buy you out is taking your idea to small and medium-sized businesses. Such firms would be happy to produce an item producing sales in amounts that simply don't interest large companies. Smaller firms may lack marketing and distribution expertise, but again your major problem is even finding one that can help you realize your idea and is interested in trying.

Will Your New Business Ideas Make Money?

This is the question that worries everybody. Here is where the risk arises that makes it so difficult to interest people in backing your idea.

It's a question that's really impossible to answer with any assurance. After all, major corporations even with massive market studies hit clinkers
all the time. Remember the Edsel? On the other hand, an idea so seemingly stupid that you'd think it was somebody's idea of a silly joke might make millions. Don't you wish you'd though of the pet rock?

So many factors need to be considered to answer this question. Is there a market? Where is it? Is it concentrated or dispersed? Could the size of the market change suddenly? Will competition drive you out? These questions are by no means the bottom of the iceberg. Yet, answering the money question to the satisfaction of potential backers is the key to the other questions.

Can You Protect Your Business Ideas?

Once you've come up with tentatively satisfying answers to the originality, production and distribution, and saleability questions, its time to consider protecting your idea. After all, looks like you may have something.

If you do have a patentable item, it's time to look into trying to protect it under the patent laws. Here briefly are the steps you'll need to follow:

Get a close friend (who understands your invention) to sign his or her name on a dated diagram or written description of the invention. Or, you can file a "disclosure document" with the Patent Office. Taking one to these measures will provide evidence of the time you came up with your invention in case of a dispute with other inventors over who conceived it first. Sending yourself a registered letter describing the invention itself is useless as evidence. Get patent protection as soon as possible.

Make a patent search to see whether or not the inventory has already been patented in as good or better version. You can make a search yourself. The only place to make such a search efficiently is at the Patent and Trademark Office in Arlington, Virginia. The staff at the Office will help you. You may find, however that the only practical way to proceed from patent search on is with the help of a patent attorney.

If the invention has not been patented, prepare a patent application and file it with the Patent and Trademark Office.

Again, you can do this yourself, following the pattern you find in similar, recent patents, though, again, a patent attorney will be helpful. If you have an attorney prepare your application, go through the exercise yourself, anyway. Compare your application with your attorney's. Make sure all of the points you regard as important are covered and that the attorney has written what you want to say. Work out differences together.

Promptly file amendments or additional patent application with the Office if you make important changes in your invention.

Having a patent won't mean you have absolute protection. In fact, one survey found that in over 70% of infringement cases brought by patent holders to protect their patents, the patent itself was held invalid.

Defending your patent can be very expensive. If you don't have a patent, however the probability of successfully protecting your invention approaches zero.

Mere ideas or suggestions can't be patented. Some of these you may be able to be put in patentable form, but for those that you can't it's pretty much do-it-yourself. Consult with a patent attorney or the Patent Office about the classes of patentable subject matter.

Say, for example, you think you have a great gimmick for selling more of Company A's products. Leaving aside the likelihood that Company A won't be interested, how do you approach Company A with your idea with any assurance they won't simply use it without paying a cent?

About the best you can do is write them a letter telling them you have a promotional (or whatever) idea and, without giving them any details, offer to send it to them. Include in your letter a statement to be signed and returned by a Company A representative promising they won't divulge your idea or make use of it without compensation (to be negotiated between them and you), if they'd like to know the details of your plan. They'll probably say thanks but no thanks or that they can't promise any such things without seeing the idea, but it's the only course open to you.

Is There Any Hope?

Each section of this Guide seems to be packed with bad news, but the Guide wouldn't be doing you any favors by raising false hopes. The point is, you need to be more than an idea person to make money out of an invention or other innovation.

Many small businesses have been doomed from the start because of false hopes. Those of you who already operate going firms have avoided wishful thinking in other business areas. You need to avoid it where innovation is concerned, too.

What are potential idea and invention backers looking for? If you read around the subject, you'll run across many comments to the effect that:

- What we want is an entrepreneur, someone who cannot only invent a product but find capital and a way of getting the product on the market.
- It's better to have a fair new product and a great manager than the other way around.
- Management is the most important element for success of an invention.

Edison wasn't only an inventing genius. He was also a promoting genius, a publicity genius, a capital-raising genius, a genius at seeing potential markets for inventions.

Have you ever heard of Joseph Swan? A strong case could be made for saying he invented the electric light eight months before Edison. Who got the patents? Who got the bulb to the market? Edison. Who invented the electric light bulb? Edison.

Few of us are Edisons. We may have brilliant product

ideas, but we aren't usually knowledgeable, let alone brilliant, in all of the areas that need to be covered. We need help.

Where Can You Go for Help?

While you probably still have to invest considerable perspiration yourself, you can get help with some of the sweating. Even Edison had some help.

Patent Attorneys and Agents

Attorneys and agents can help you make patent searches and applications, if you can't do them yourself. The U.S. Patent Office has geographical and alphabetical listings of such people, but doesn't make recommendations or assume any responsibility for your selection from their lists. You can also find attorneys and agents by looking in the classified section of your telephone directory under "Patents."

Invention Promotion Firms

Also likely to be listed in the "Patents" section of the directory are firms that offer - for a fee- to take on the whole job of protecting and promoting your idea. Caution is necessary in dealing with such promoters.

Federal Trade Commission investigations found that one firm, which charged fees ranging from $1,000 to $2,000 had ten clients who made money on their inventions - that was out of a total of 35,000. Another firm with 30,000 had only three with successful inventions. If you elect to use an idea promotion firm, make sure:

- They don't collect the entire fee in advance.
- They will provide you with samples of their promotional materials and lists of companies to whom they've sent it. (Then check with those companies yourself.)
- You check the promotion firm's reputation with the local Better Business Bureau, Chamber of Commerce, a patent attorney, or a local inventors or innovators club.

Invention Brokers

Brokers work for a portion of the profits from an invention. They may help inventors raise capital and form companies to produce and market their inventions. They often provide sophisticated management advice. In general, you can expect these brokers to be interested in more complex technology with fairly large sales potential.

University Innovation/Invention/Entrepreneurial Centers

These centers, some funded by the National Science Foundation, show promise for helping inventors and innovators. The best known one, the University of Oregon's Experimental Center for the Advancement of Invention and Innovation (The Innovation Center no longer exists), for example, evaluated an idea for a very modest fee. The Center evaluated an idea on 33 criteria (listed earlier in this Guide) to help inventors weed out bad ideas so they won't waste further time and money on them.

The Center also identified trouble spots that required special attention in planning the development or commercialization of a potential new product. If an idea looked like it had merit and was commercially feasible, the Center tried to link the innovator with established companies or referred him or her to sources of funds.

Inventor's Clubs/Associations/Societies

You may have such clubs in your locality. You can share experiences with kindred spirits and get good advice, low cost evaluation, and other help.

Talking with other inventors is probably the most helpful thing you can do. Find someone who has been through the entire routine of patents, applied R & D, and stages of financing. It doesn't matter if the end result was a financial success or failure. Getting the nitty-gritty of the process is what's important.

Are You Being Unreasonable About Your Chances?

If you have read this Guide and still think you can make money with your idea, some people might think you've missed the point. If you continue to believe in your idea after looking at the odds and obstacles, you are being unreasonable.

That's exactly what you should be. You're in good company.

All progress is made by unreasonable people. George Bernard Shaw observed: Reasonable people adapt to the world around them, unreasonable people try to change it.

17. Special Free Bonuses (download links are provided)

a. Excel Financial Projections Creator - simply type in your business' details and assumptions and it will automatically produce a comprehensive set of financial projections for your specific business, including: Start-Up Expenses, Projected Balance Sheet, Projected Cash Flow Statement, Financial Ratios Analysis, Projected Profit and Loss Statement, Break Even Analysis, and many more.

Copy the following link to your browser and save the file to your PC:

http://www.bizmove.com/bp/projections.xlsx

b. Detailed guide that will walk you step by step and show you exactly how to effectively use the above Excel Financial Projections Creator.

Copy the following link to your browser and save the file to your PC:

http://www.bizmove.com/bp/projections-guide.doc

c. How to Improve Your Leadership and Management Skills (eBook) - Discover powerful strategies to motivate and inspire your people to bring out the best in them. Be the boss people want to give 200 percent for.

Copy the following link to your browser and save the file to your PC:

http://www.bizmove.com/bp/leadership.pdf

d. Small Business Management: Essential Ingredients for Success (eBook) - Learn effective business management tricks, secrets and shortcuts to make your business a success.

Copy the following link to your browser and save the file to your PC:

http://www.bizmove.com/bp/management.pdf

e. How To Gain A Competitive Advantage - Training Course (Online Video) - What sets you apart from your competition? Learn how to get a competitive advantage with this course. Learn how to brand, study your competition, identify customers and their preferences, create pricing strategies and much more. Leverage the uniqueness of your business to create a real competitive advantage.

Copy the following link to your browser and save the file to your PC:

http://www.bizmove.com/business-training/how-to-gain-a-competitive-advantage.htm

f. How To Finance a Business (Online Video Training Course) - This self-paced training exercise is an introduction to financing options for your business. Topics include; determining your financial needs, loans, grants, venture capital, angel investors, crowd funding and other financial options available to small businesses.

Copy the following link to your browser and save the file to your PC:

http://www.bizmove.com/business-training/how-to-finance-a-business.htm

www.ingramcontent.com/pod-product-compliance
Lightning Source LLC
Chambersburg PA
CBHW071221220526
45468CB00002B/695